WHISTLING SWAN

Swans and *Wild Geese*

Illustrated by Marie Nonnast Bohlen

MUTE SWAN
AND CYGNETS

BRANT

Swans *and* Wild Geese

Written *by* *Edwin A. Mason*

TRUMPETER SWAN

CANADA GOOSE

BLUE GOOSE

FOLLETT PUBLISHING COMPANY
CHICAGO

ISBN 0-695-48385-4 Titan binding
ISBN 0-695-88385-2 Trade binding

Library of Congress Catalog Card Number: 69-15767

First Printing G

Copy 1

To the "Givers,"
who made possible a peaceful home
for the
American continent's waterfowl:
the ducks and the
even more spectacular
swans and wild geese.

BLUE GOOSE

6

CANADA GOOSE

SNOW GOOSE

Blue skies, shallow waters, golden-green grasses swaying in the winds. This is the world of swans and geese. They are the largest of waterbirds, and they make their homes in marshes, along the shores of lakes and rivers, and in shallow, salty waters along the sea shores.

WHISTLING SWAN

WHITE-FRONTED GOOSE

BLUE GOOSE

TRUMPETER SWAN

WHITE-FRONTED GOOSE

BRANT

CANADA GOOSE

Swans and geese are close relatives. The swans have longer necks than geese, and are usually larger. Adult swans of the northern parts of the world are mostly white, with younger birds having a grayish look. Australia has a beautiful black swan.

AUSTRALIAN BLACK SWAN

WHISTLING SWAN

10   Men have loved the grace and beauty of swans from the earliest days. Many songs and stories have been created about these birds.

HANS CHRISTIAN ANDERSEN'S, "THE WILD SWANS"

The wild swan seen most often in North America is the **11** whistling swan. It has a black bill, with yellow below the eyes, and holds its head level as it swims. Its cry is more like the notes of a flute than like a whistle, and it can sound many different notes.

WHISTLING SWAN

12   Whistling swans raise their young in wild places of northern North America. Their marshland nests are very large and usually contain about six eggs.

WHISTLING SWAN

Newly hatched swans, called cygnets (SIG-nets), are a light gray color. The parents take very good care of their babies, leading them to the water and teaching them to eat bits of plants and tiny water animals, very soon after they are hatched.

WHISTLING SWAN
AND CYGNETS

14   Swans eat leaves, roots, and seeds, as well as insects, water
creatures, and even small land animals such as lizards. The
long necks of the birds are useful as they search around
on the bottoms of the ponds.

WHISTLING SWAN

Both male and female swans help care for the young. They defend the cygnets fiercely if an enemy comes, pecking and using their powerful wings as weapons. People who eat swans' eggs as part of their diet risk broken bones when gathering them. Few animal enemies dare to attack an adult swan.

WHISTLING SWAN

16   When the short northern summer ends, whistling swans travel southward, or migrate, often in a single line. They go into places in southern Canada and the United States where they find unfrozen water to swim in all through the winter. In spring, they return to their arctic homes to nest.

WHISTLING SWAN

The trumpeter swan, larger than the whistler, is the largest of all North American waterfowl. Its wings spread nearly eight feet. It has a tiny pinkish strip at the base of its black beak. Trumpeters have loud voices that sound something like a French horn and may be heard more than a mile away.

TRUMPETER SWAN

Trumpeter swans are very rare now, as hunters killed thousands for food, sport, and for the breast feathers, known as swansdown. Now they may be seen in Yellowstone National Park and Canada, where they are protected from hunters.

The mute, or voiceless, swan of Europe was first placed in
American park lakes as a decoration. It escaped and be-
came wild. Now these birds nest along the Atlantic coast.
Most "tame" swans in city parks and zoos are mute swans.
Look for a bird with an orange-colored beak and a neck
held in a graceful curve while swimming.

MUTE SWAN

20

CANADIAN HONKER

RICHARDSON'S
CANADA GOOSE

CACKLING CANADA GOOSE

The best-known wild goose is the Canada goose, a beautiful bird far different from the fat, tame geese that were once common in farmyards. Its body feathers are gray with lighter edges. The long neck and head are black, and there is a light-colored "chinstrap" of feathers around the throat. Canada geese do not all look alike. They may be of different sizes and have different shades of gray feathers.

WESTERN CANADA GOOSE

ALEUTIAN CANADA GOOSE

22 Seeds, grain, and greenery are the main food of the Canada goose. Once these birds lived mostly on wild food. But today they eat a great deal of grain such as wheat and rice from the farmers' fields. They also graze on growing grain during the winter months.

CANADA GOOSE

As the birds feed, guards watch for animal enemies. The geese are so alert that nothing can get near the flock unseen. Human beings find geese delicious, and hunters take many every year. Wise hunting laws see to it that the number of nesting birds does not get too low. Wild geese become fewer when their nesting places are taken over for human use.

CANADA GOOSE

Male and female geese mate for life. It is said that if one of the pair is killed, the other may never mate again. The goose and gander build a nest out of reeds, grass and soft down feathers plucked from their breasts. Six or seven eggs are laid, which hatch into lively goslings after about 28 days.

The goslings swim about with their mother, learning to eat plant food and avoid their enemies. Mink and snapping turtles sometimes catch the goslings.

CANADA GOOSE AND GOSLINGS

During the summer, while the goslings are still young, the parent geese molt or lose their worn-out feathers, slowly growing new ones. The goslings also lose their baby down and grow adult feathers. By the time fall comes, both parents and their grown-up young are ready to fly south as the days shorten and deep cold flows down from the polar lands.

CANADA GOOSE AND GOSLINGS

Canada geese often migrate in V-shaped flocks, traveling from Canada and the northern United States southward to the Gulf states and other warm places where there is plenty of food. They seek places far away from people, their greatest single enemy.

CANADA GOOSE

28

SNOW GOOSE

Several other kinds of wild geese live in North America. All have long necks, short, strong legs, and powerful wings. The handsome white snow geese have black tips on their wings. When flying, they are sometimes mistaken for swans; but their necks are much shorter.

The common snow goose builds its nest in the far North and spends the winters on lakes and seacoasts farther south. A smaller kind of snow goose lives in the West.

30 Brants look much like Canada geese, but they are smaller and do not have white cheek patches. These wild geese breed in the Arctic. The American brant winters in the bays and sounds of the Atlantic Coast and also is found in inland marshes. The black brant winters on the Pacific Coast.

AMERICAN BRANT

BLACK BRANT

Some other North American geese are the blue goose, which is really gray with a white head, and the white-fronted or laughing goose with dark streaks on its breast. One of the most handsome geese is the emperor goose, which lives in the Alaskan islands during the winter and nests in the far North. Not much is known about its life because it nests far from human beings.

WHITE-FRONTED GOOSE

EMPEROR GOOSE

BLUE GOOSE

The governments of both the United States and Canada care for swans and geese as they migrate to and from nesting places and winter homes. Refuges and sanctuaries, where the birds are safe from hunters, have been set up. If laws protecting the birds can be made to work, there will always be wild swans and geese for us to enjoy.